Jesus Is the Same: Living in the Power of an Unchanging Savior.

Goitsemodimo Mafasola

Acknowledgements

Writing this book has been a journey of faith, perseverance, and grace, and I could not have done it alone.

First and foremost, I give thanks to my Lord and Savior, Jesus Christ. Your love, wisdom, and guidance have been my source of inspiration throughout this process. To You be all the glory for the message within these pages.

To my beloved wife, Tidimalo Brenda Mafasola and children, thank you for your unwavering support and sacrifices during the long hours of writing and ministry. Your encouragement has been my greatest strength.

I extend my heartfelt gratitude to the congregation of Apostolic Sword of the Spirit International Church. Your prayers, testimonies, and hunger for God's Word have inspired many of the reflections shared in this book.

To Apostle JB Makananisa, leader of Charis Missionary Church and my father in the Lord, thank you for your teachings, mentorship, and the powerful example you set as a servant of God. Your words of wisdom and impartation have profoundly shaped my journey in ministry and life.

Special thanks to my mentors and instructors at Christian Leaders Institute, who have played a pivotal role in my growth as a minister. Your teaching and example have been invaluable.

To my editors and reviewers, thank you for helping refine and polish this work. Your insights and dedication have brought clarity and depth to the message.

Lastly, I am profoundly grateful for every reader of this book. My prayer is that these words touch your heart, strengthen your faith, and draw you closer to the Bread of Life, Jesus Christ.

May God bless each one of you abundantly.

Introduction: The Unchanging Savior

"Jesus Christ is the same yesterday, today, and forever." – Hebrews 13:8

Life is unpredictable. Seasons change, circumstances shift, and we often find ourselves grappling with uncertainty. In the midst of it all, one truth remains constant: Jesus Christ is unchanging. The same Savior who healed the sick, raised the dead, and calmed the storms over 2,000 years ago is alive and active today.

But do we believe it?

Too often, we limit our expectations of what Jesus can do. We box Him into our past experiences or relegate His power to the pages of scripture. Yet, the Jesus who walked on water and fed thousands is the same Jesus who walks with us through our struggles, provides for our needs, and heals our brokenness today.

This book is a journey through the stories of people who encountered the unchanging Savior. From a desperate father pleading for his daughter's life to a woman who reached out in faith, their lives were transformed by Jesus' power. These stories are not just ancient accounts; they are reflections of what He can and will do in our lives.

My prayer is that as you read, your faith will be renewed and your heart awakened to the reality that Jesus is as present and powerful now as He has ever been. Let's step into the fullness of His unchanging love and grace together.

Table of Contents

Chapter 1: Faith in Crisis   1

Chapter 2: The God of Now and Eternity   8

Chapter 4: The Power of Persistent Faith   22

Chapter 5: A Touch of Faith   31

Chapter 6: The Bread of Life   38

Chapter 7: Walking on Water   41

Chapter 8: Living Water   46

Chapter 9: The Vine and the Branches   52

Chapter 10: The Power of the Resurrection   59

Chapter 1: Faith in Crisis

"Don't be afraid; just believe." – Mark 5:36

Jairus was desperate. His daughter, just twelve years old, lay dying. He had exhausted every option, but nothing could save her. In an act of faith, he sought out Jesus, throwing himself at the feet of the only One who could help.

On the way to Jairus' house, the crowd pressed in, slowing their progress. Suddenly, Jesus stopped. "Who touched me?" He asked. His disciples were incredulous. With so many people jostling around Him, how could He ask such a question? But Jesus knew. A woman, suffering from a twelve-year-long illness, had reached out in faith and touched His garment. Instantly, she was healed.

Imagine Jairus' turmoil at that moment. Time was running out, and now this interruption might cost his daughter's life. Then came the dreaded news: "Your daughter is dead. Why bother the teacher anymore?"

But Jesus turned to Jairus and spoke words that resonate through the ages: *"Don't be afraid; just believe."*

When they arrived at Jairus' house, mourners filled the air with weeping.

Jesus entered the room, took the child's hand, and said, *"Little girl, I say to you, get up!"* Immediately, she rose, and the once-grieving house was filled with joy.

When Faith Meets Desperation

There is something about the intersection of faith and desperation that brings out the very best in us. When everything seems lost, when we have nowhere else to turn, it is in those moments that we often find God moving in the most miraculous ways. Jairus' faith in the face of his crisis is a powerful reminder that even when it seems like all hope is gone, Jesus is still able to turn things around.

This was not just a story of physical healing; it was a story of faith in crisis. Jairus had nothing left but his faith, and it was that faith that led to the resurrection of his daughter. His faith did not prevent the crisis from happening, but it enabled him to trust in the presence and power of Jesus, even in the midst of the most devastating news.

Faith often grows strongest in our moments of greatest need. Jairus' story in Mark 5 is a testament to this truth, but so is my own.

In 2015, I found myself unemployed, living in a rented one-room house with a single P10 note left to my name. The end of the month loomed, and I had no money for rent or food beyond a bottle of peanut butter. My circumstances felt impossibly bleak. One Saturday morning, overwhelmed by my situation, I knelt in prayer. With a heavy heart, I cried out to God, asking for a sign that He was there and that He could provide for me. I was honest with Him about my need—a financial breakthrough. After pouring out my heart, I went back to bed, still holding on to hope but unsure of what the day would bring.

An hour later, my phone rang. It was an unknown number. A woman on the other end explained that she was looking for a Setswana facilitator—a role I had worked in the previous year. She wanted to meet that same day to discuss the opportunity. My P10 note became my lifeline, covering the fare to meet her. By the time our meeting ended, I had secured a job, received a P100 note, and walked away with bags of leftover food from a party she had hosted the night before—pizza, fruit, and more than enough to sustain me.

That day, I knew without a shadow of a doubt that God hears prayers and provides. He is never late, and His faithfulness is unwavering.

Reflection

- What situation in your life feels like it's "too late" for Jesus to intervene?

- How can you take the step of faith to trust Him, even when fear says otherwise?

In Jairus' story, we see a powerful lesson about the intersection of faith and crisis. Jesus didn't promise that the crisis wouldn't come, but He did promise that He would be with us in the midst of it. Jairus chose to believe, even when everything around him pointed to despair. His faith was rewarded with a miracle that defied logic, time, and circumstance.

When we face our own crises, may we have the courage to hear Jesus' words: **"Don't be afraid; just believe."** The answer to our crisis is not found in our own strength or understanding but in trusting in the One who has the power to bring life out of death, to make a way where there seems to be no way.

Takeaway:

Faith in crisis is not about pretending the storm isn't real; it's about trusting that Jesus has the power to calm it. When we trust Him in the midst of our struggles, we open the door for miracles. Just as Jairus' faith led to the resurrection of his daughter, our faith, even in the darkest of times, can bring about the miraculous hand of God.

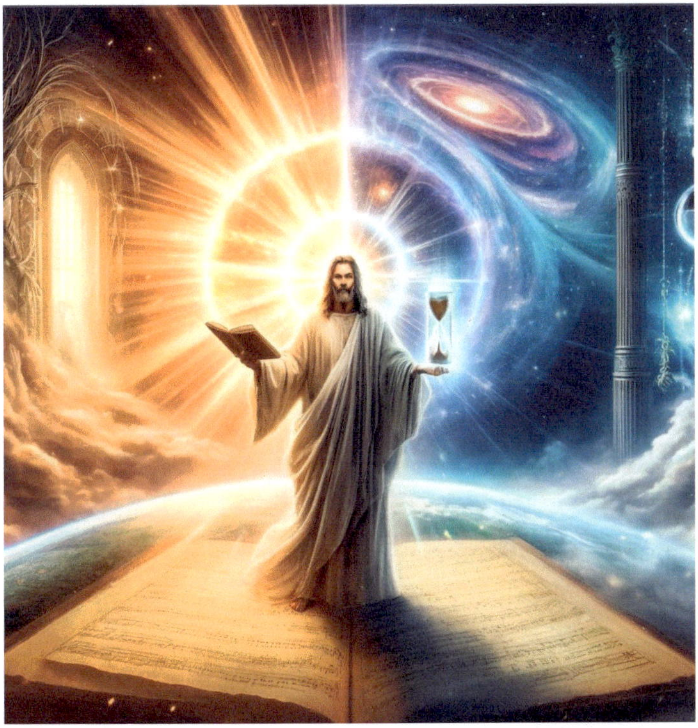

Chapter 2: The God of Now and Eternity

"I am the resurrection and the life. The one who believes in me will live, even though they die." – John 11:25

Have you ever found yourself asking God, *"Why didn't You show up sooner?"* Mary and Martha asked this very question when their brother Lazarus fell ill and Jesus delayed coming to them. They knew He could heal, but their faith was bound by what they had seen Him do before. They believed in His power for the future but struggled to see His ability to move in the present.

Lazarus died, and by the time Jesus arrived, he had been in the tomb for four days (John 11:17). Grief hung heavy in the air. Both sisters echoed the same words when they saw Jesus: *"Lord, if You had been here, my brother would not have died"* (John 11:21, 32).

Their faith was not absent, but it was incomplete. Martha believed in a future resurrection, saying, *"I know he will rise again in the resurrection at the last day"* (John 11:24), and Mary mourned the past wishing that Jesus had arrived sooner to heal her brother. Neither fully grasped that Jesus was present and powerful in that very moment. Neither fully understood that the same Jesus, the one they were waiting for in the future, was standing right in front of them. He was not bound by time. He was the resurrection, and He was present—right then.

Jesus, the Resurrection and the Life

Jesus didn't just speak of resurrection as a distant event; He declared it as His identity. *"I am the resurrection and the life,"* He told Martha (John 11:25). This wasn't just a theological statement—it was a declaration that the power of life itself rested in Him.

Standing before the tomb, Jesus wept (John 11:35). Then He prayed and called out with authority: *"Lazarus, come out!"* (John 11:43). And Lazarus, once bound by death, walked out alive (John 11:44).

This miracle was more than a restoration of life; it was a revelation of Jesus' divine authority over time and circumstance. He is not limited by the "too late" or the "not yet." He is the God of now.

The power to bring life to the dead was not just something He could do—it was Who He was. He can break through any situation, no matter how long it's been, how impossible it seems, or how "too late" we feel.

My Lazarus Moment

The story of Lazarus resonates deeply because I've experienced moments where hope seemed lost, only for Jesus to step in and reveal His power.

One such moment happened during a Sunday service. A child, no older than four years old, collapsed during worship. Panic swept through the congregation. Mothers cried, and fear filled the air, but the church rallied in prayer. We cried out to God as one body, trusting in His ability to bring life. To the amazement of everyone, the child was restored, breathing again, and peace returned to what had been a scene of chaos. It was a powerful reminder that Jesus, the resurrection and the life, is present even in our moments of deepest fear.

Another time, our church faced an overwhelming financial challenge around March 2024. We had set a date to build a church structure, but the funds required—over 24,000 pula—seemed far beyond our reach. With just two weeks to go, no significant pledges or contributions had come in. Feeling the weight of the situation, we gathered at the church grounds as intercessors and believers to pray for provision.

Miraculously, by the end of the first week, we had raised 6,000 pula. By the second week, another 12,000 pula came in—donations from both members and non-members. Even more astounding was what happened during the building weekend. A couple from the UK, visiting Botswana at the time, saw the incomplete structure and bought the additional supplies we needed right on the spot.

These moments were not coincidences; they were divine interventions. Jesus stepped into what seemed like insurmountable obstacles and provided life, provision, and restoration. Just as He called Lazarus from the grave, He continues to call us out of our "impossible" situations and into His abundance.

Faith Beyond the Future

Too often, we confine Jesus' power to the future. We believe He'll save us in eternity but struggle to trust Him with the now. Mary and Martha's story reminds us that Jesus operates beyond our timelines and expectations. His power is as relevant today as it was in Bethany.

He is not bound by the "not yet" or the "too late." He is the God who works in the present moment, no matter the circumstances. His power is not just for the future—it is for today.

Just as Jesus called Lazarus out of the tomb, He calls us out of our own tombs of despair, fear, and hopelessness. He calls us to believe not just in a distant future, but in the power He has to act in our lives *now*. Whatever situation feels too late, too impossible, or too far gone, remember: Jesus is the resurrection and the life. He can act today.

Reflection
- Where have you limited Jesus to the "not yet"?
- What is one situation you can bring to Him in faith, believing He can act today?

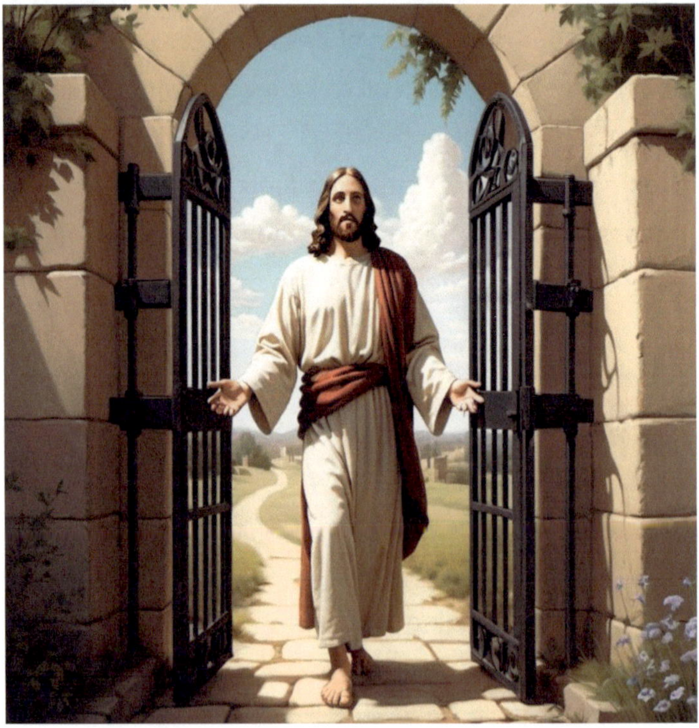

Chapter 3: Jesus at the Gate

"Go home to your own people and tell them how much the Lord has done for you, and how he has had mercy on you." – Mark 5:19

Jesus' power to transform lives is vividly displayed in the story of the man at the gates of Gadara. Known as the Gerasene demoniac, his life was a picture of torment and isolation. Possessed by a legion of demons, he lived among the tombs, an outcast from society and a prisoner of his mind (Mark 5:2-5). Yet, one encounter with Jesus changed everything. This chapter explores how Jesus brings freedom, restoration, and purpose, even in the most hopeless situations. It also reflects on moments in my ministry where I've seen Jesus at work in similar ways.

Freedom from Bondage

When Jesus arrived in the region of the Gerasenes, the man ran to Him and fell at His feet (Mark 5:6). Though the demons cried out in fear, Jesus commanded them to leave, sending them into a herd of pigs that rushed into the sea (Mark 5:11-13).

What strikes me most about this story is the immediate transformation. The man who was once uncontrollable, cutting himself and crying out night and day, was now sitting clothed and in his right mind (Mark 5:15).

This kind of freedom is not theoretical. I've witnessed Jesus break chains of addiction, restore fractured families, and heal minds plagued by torment. One instance involved a young woman battling addiction and identity confusion. Through counseling and prayer, she found freedom, returned to school, and began to rebuild her life.

Restoration of Dignity

The townspeople were afraid of the man's transformation. They asked Jesus to leave, unable to comprehend the power they had just witnessed (Mark 5:17). But Jesus' work didn't end there. He restored the man's dignity by giving him a purpose.

When the man begged to go with Jesus, He told him instead to return home and testify: *"Go home to your own people and tell them how much the Lord has done for you"* (Mark 5:19). This once-ostracized individual became a witness of God's mercy and power, proclaiming the gospel throughout the Decapolis (Mark 5:20).

I've seen similar stories in our church. One unforgettable testimony involved a mother who requested prayer for her daughter studying in China. The young woman had experienced severe health challenges, initially requiring crutches to walk. Her condition worsened until she was confined to a wheelchair.

One Sunday, the mother came to the church, burdened with concern. As a congregation, we prayed with fervent faith. Thousands of miles away, the daughter experienced a miraculous healing. She was completely restored and able to walk again without any aid. Her studies continued without interruption, and beyond physical healing, God worked in her situation financially and administratively. She received a smooth visa renewal process and financial stability, showcasing Jesus' comprehensive power to restore every area of life.

This miracle illustrated the power of Jesus to restore all areas of our lives—health, provision, and even purpose. The mother's testimony became a powerful reminder that God is not bound by distance or circumstance. He can transform lives, no matter the situation.

Jesus at Our Gate

Like the man at Gadara, we all face battles—some external, others internal. But Jesus is always at the gate, ready to intervene. His power to restore isn't confined to biblical accounts; it's alive and active today.

There have been times in ministry when I've felt like we were standing at a spiritual gate, facing obstacles that seemed insurmountable. One such moment came when we needed resources to expand our outreach programs. Through prayer and faith, we not only received the necessary support but also witnessed lives transformed as a result of those efforts.

Reflection

Jesus is the same yesterday, today, and forever. His power to free us from bondage, restore our dignity, and give us purpose is still alive and active today. He stands at the gates of our lives, waiting for us to invite Him in.

- **What gates in your life are you asking Jesus to step through?**

    Consider the areas of your life where you feel trapped, isolated, or burdened. Is there a part of your heart that has been given over to fear, anger, or addiction? Jesus is ready to step in and bring freedom.

- **How can you testify to what He has already done for you?**

    Take time to reflect on the ways God has already intervened in your life. Whether it was physical healing, emotional restoration, or a breakthrough in a difficult situation, share your story with others. Your testimony is powerful and can bring hope to those who are facing similar struggles.

Just as Jesus transformed the life of the man at Gadara, He is ready to transform yours. All we need to do is come to Him, surrender our lives, and watch as He works miracles in and through us.

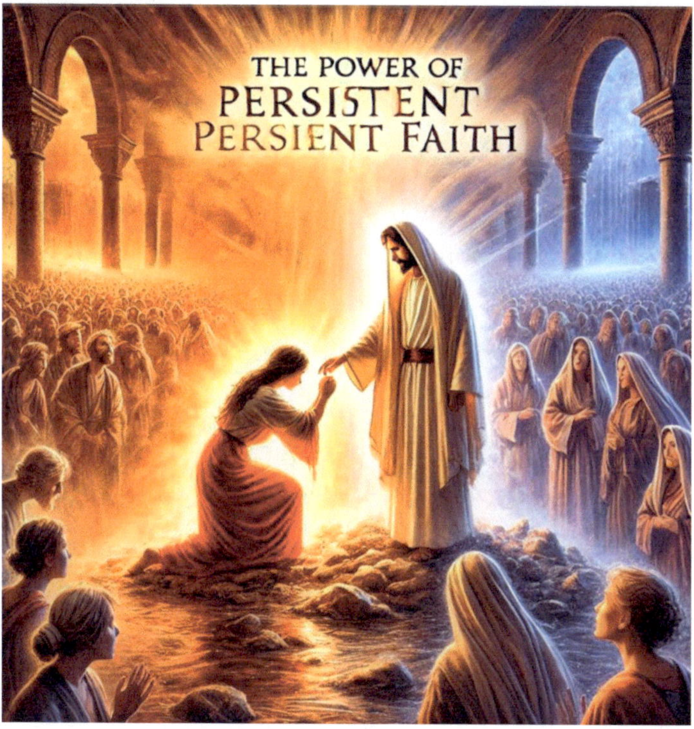
THE POWER OF
PERSISTENT
PERSIENT FAITH

Chapter 4: The Power of Persistent Faith

"Then Jesus said to her, 'Woman, you have great faith! Your request is granted.' And her daughter was healed at that moment." – Matthew 15:28
"Daughter, your faith has healed you. Go in peace and be freed from your suffering." – Mark 5:34

Faith is not passive; it is a persistent force that pushes through barriers, silence, and even rejection. In Matthew 15 and Mark 5, two women demonstrate this kind of faith—faith that would not give up. These stories not only highlight the tenacity of their faith but also demonstrate how persistent faith can turn hopeless situations into miraculous victories. Their stories, combined with testimonies from my ministry, reveal how faith can transform hopeless situations into miraculous victories.

A Mother's Plea: Faith in the Face of Silence

The Syrophoenician woman's story in Matthew 15:21-28 begins with her desperate plea for her demon-possessed daughter. At first, Jesus did not respond. Even His disciples suggested she be sent away. Yet, she remained undeterred.

When Jesus finally addressed her, saying, *"It is not right to take the children's bread and toss it to the dogs"* (Matthew 15:26), her humility and determination shone: *"Even the dogs eat the crumbs that fall from their master's table"* (Matthew 15:27). This act of persistent faith moved Jesus, and He granted her request, healing her daughter instantly.

The lesson here is clear: Persistent faith is not dissuaded by initial silence or rejection. It recognizes the power of Jesus, even when circumstances or words seem to suggest otherwise. This kind of faith does not demand immediate answers but trusts in God's ability to respond in His perfect timing.

A Woman's Touch: Faith That Reaches Out

Mark 5:25-34 recounts the story of a woman who had suffered from a bleeding condition for 12 years. She had exhausted all her resources seeking help but only grew worse. Socially isolated and considered ceremonially unclean, she defied societal norms to press through the crowd and touch the hem of Jesus' garment.

Her faith was so potent that Jesus immediately noticed power leave Him. When she revealed herself, trembling with fear, He reassured her: *"Daughter, your faith has healed you. Go in peace and be freed from your suffering"* (Mark 5:34).

Her faith was active and bold. She didn't wait for Jesus to come to her or give a direct invitation. She believed that her act of reaching out would bring her healing, and it did. Her faith, though small in action, was great in belief.

Modern-Day Miracles: Persistent Prayer at Work

These stories came alive in our ministry through real-life testimonies.

For instance the story of a mother sought prayer for her daughter, who was in China. The young woman had been battling severe health issues, transitioning from crutches to a wheelchair. The situation seemed hopeless, but we prayed with unwavering faith.

That week, thousands of miles away, the daughter experienced a miraculous healing. She regained her ability to walk, saw her finances restored, and had her visa renewal process go smoothly.

Similarly, like the woman who pressed through the crowd, our church faced a seemingly insurmountable challenge when trying to build a new structure. Financial resources were scarce, and the deadline loomed. We turned to God in prayer, believing for provision.

Over the next two weeks, donations began to pour in from unexpected sources, including a couple visiting from the UK who bought additional supplies when they saw the incomplete structure. By the time the project was finished, we stood in awe of what God had done.

Lessons in Faith

Both women in scripture faced rejection, isolation, and delay, yet their faith remained steadfast. They teach us that persistent faith breaks barriers—be it cultural norms, physical limitations, or spiritual obstacles.

As the Syrophoenician woman shows us, faith must remain determined even when faced with silence. As the woman with the issue of blood demonstrates, faith requires action, pressing through the crowd to touch Jesus.

Their stories teach us powerful lessons about persistent faith:

- **Faith Breaks Barriers**:

Whether societal norms, physical limitations, or spiritual obstacles, persistent faith refuses to be held back. The Syrophoenician woman was a Gentile, an outsider in Jewish society, yet her faith reached beyond cultural boundaries and received Jesus' favor.

- **Faith Requires Action**:

Like the woman who pressed through the crowd to touch Jesus' garment, faith is not passive. It requires movement. It's not enough to believe; we must take steps that align with our belief and trust that God will meet us there.

- **Faith Stands Firm in Silence and Delay**:

Both women were initially met with silence and delay, yet their faith never wavered. We are reminded that God's timing is not our own, and while He may seem silent, He is always at work behind the scenes.

Reflection

- **Are there areas in your life where you've given up too soon?**

  Examine areas where you may have lost hope. Have you given up on a dream, a prayer, or a situation because of silence or delays? Let this be a reminder to press on in faith, even when the answer seems long in coming.

- **What steps can you take today to exercise persistent faith in God's promises?**

  Think about one area where you need to exercise persistent faith. What is one step you can take today that aligns your actions with your belief? Whether it's continuing in prayer, trusting God for provision, or stepping out in boldness, let this be the day you commit to a faith that perseveres.

Faith for Today

Faith is not just believing; it is acting in alignment with that belief. Whether you are praying for healing, provision, or restoration, remember that Jesus is the same yesterday, today, and forever (Hebrews 13:8).

The same power that healed and restored in these biblical stories is available to you. Just as the two women persisted in faith and saw miracles, so can we experience the same breakthroughs in our lives today.

Persistent faith does not just wait for God to act; it trusts that God is already at work, moving behind the scenes, and calls us to walk by faith in every situation.

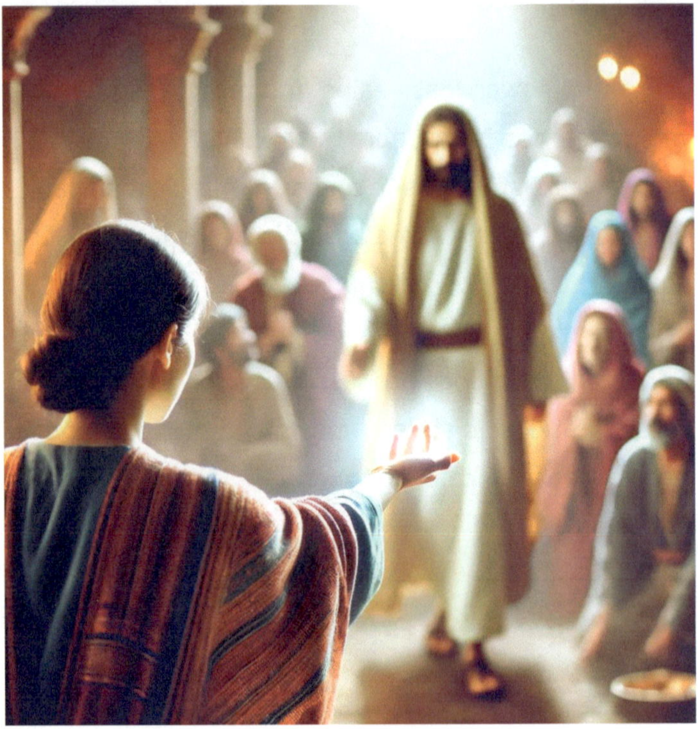

Chapter 5: A Touch of Faith

"If I only touch his cloak, I will be healed." –
Matthew 9:21

Faith is often thought of as grand declarations or monumental acts, but sometimes, it is as simple and profound as a single touch. This chapter explores the transformative power of faith expressed through a touch—whether it is reaching out to Jesus, touching others in compassion, or allowing God's touch to heal and restore. The simple yet powerful act of faith through touch can bring profound change to our lives.

The Faith That Reaches Out

The story of the woman with the issue of blood, as recounted in Matthew 9:20-22 and Mark 5:25-34, epitomizes the power of a touch grounded in faith. For twelve years, this woman suffered immensely. She was not only physically weak but socially ostracized due to the nature of her condition. Yet, her faith ignited a boldness within her.

Believing that just touching Jesus' cloak would bring healing, she pressed through the crowd despite the societal norms that deemed her unworthy. In that moment of contact, Jesus felt power flow from Him. Her faith, expressed through the simplicity of her touch, had made her whole.

Jesus turned to her, saying, *"Take heart, daughter; your faith has healed you."* This moment teaches us that even when we feel weak or insignificant, a single act of faith can draw us closer to God and unleash His power in our lives.

Faith That Touches Others

Faith isn't only about reaching out for what we need; it is also about touching the lives of others with God's love and compassion. Jesus Himself demonstrated this throughout His ministry. When He touched the leper in Matthew 8:1-4, He didn't just heal the man physically—He restored his dignity, shattered cultural barriers, and affirmed his value.

Similarly, when Jesus touched Peter's mother-in-law in Matthew 8:14-15, the fever left her instantly, and she got up and served Him. These encounters show us that faith-filled touches are acts of restoration, compassion, and transformation.

In our lives, we are called to be the hands of Christ, extending His love and healing to those around us. A kind word, a helping hand, or even a literal touch on the shoulder can be a conduit for God's grace.

God's Touch in Our Lives

The most transformative touch of all is when God touches our hearts and lives. In moments of despair, confusion, or brokenness, His touch restores, heals, and renews. One of the most vivid examples of God's touch is found in the Old Testament, when Isaiah, confronted with God's holiness, cried out in unworthiness. An angel touched his lips with a live coal, signifying cleansing and preparation for service (Isaiah 6:6-7).

God's touch prepares us for His purpose, setting us apart and empowering us to live out our faith boldly.

In my own ministry, I have seen countless examples of lives touched by God in profound ways—addictions broken, families restored, and healing taking place in unexpected ways.

One particular story stands out: A young lady who had been battling depression and recurring headaches came to one of our services. During a moment of prayer, she described feeling as if a hand had rested on her shoulder, though no one was physically there. She later testified that in that moment, she felt a peace she had never experienced before and was freed from her struggles with self-harm. God's touch transformed her life, and she now serves as a leader in our youth ministry.

Reflections on Faith's Touch

Faith is not just about grand gestures; sometimes, it is about the simple, deliberate act of reaching out. Like the woman with the issue of blood, are there areas in your life where you need to press through the crowd of doubt, fear, or shame to touch Jesus?

- **Have you allowed God's touch to bring healing and renewal to your life?**

    Reflect on areas where you need God's touch—whether it's physical healing, emotional restoration, or spiritual renewal.

- **Are you extending faith-filled touches to others?**

    Look for opportunities to be a vessel of God's love. Who in your life needs encouragement, support, or a reminder of God's grace?

Faith in Action: Reach Out

Faith often requires action, even in its simplest form. Whether it's touching the hem of His garment, reaching out to someone in need, or allowing God to touch your heart, these small acts can have eternal impact. Let this chapter remind you of the power of faith expressed through a touch—a power that can heal, restore, and transform.

Prayer of Faith:

Lord, I come to You in faith, believing in the power of Your touch. Help me to press through every obstacle that keeps me from You. May Your touch bring healing, renewal, and restoration to my life. Use me, Lord, to extend Your touch to others, that they too may experience Your love and power. Amen.

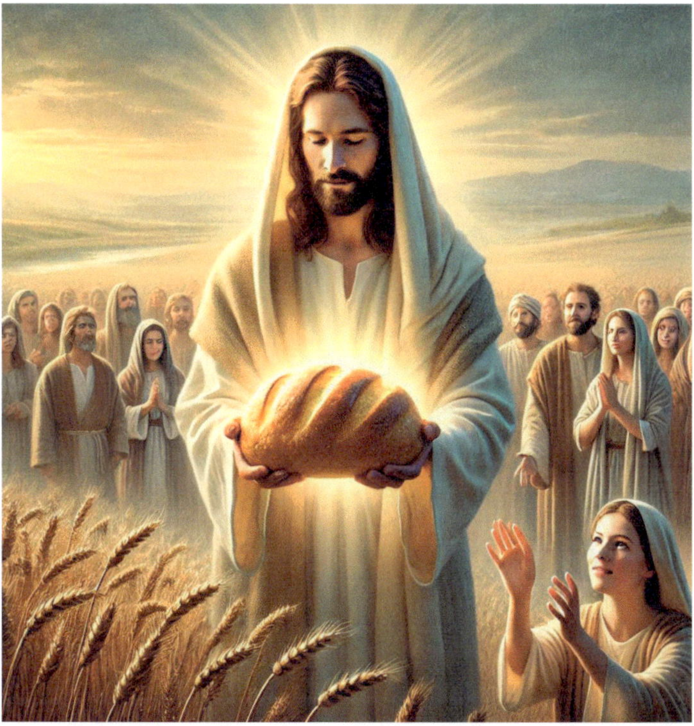

Chapter 6: The Bread of Life

Faith not only heals and restores; it nourishes. Jesus' miracles of provision remind us that He is not limited by resources or circumstances. He declares in John 6:35, *"I am the bread of life. Whoever comes to me will never go hungry, and whoever believes in me will never be thirsty."*

This chapter dives into how Jesus meets our physical and spiritual needs through miraculous provision, emphasizing His sufficiency in every situation.

The Miracle of Multiplication
The feeding of the 5,000 (John 6:1-13) is one of the most vivid illustrations of Jesus' provision. With just five loaves and two fish, He fed a multitude. This wasn't a feast prepared by human hands but a divine display of abundance. The disciples saw limitations; Jesus saw opportunity.

This same principle is alive today. In moments when we lack resources, Jesus invites us to bring what we have, however small it seems, and place it in His hands.

Testimony of Provision in the Wilderness: Jesus as the Bread of Life

My testimony about my 2015 experience, where God provided for my needs in as little as an hour (as shared in Chapter 1: *Faith in Crisis*), truly highlights the reality that Jesus is the Bread of Life.

In that season of lack, when I had only P10 left to my name and no food to eat, I turned to prayer. I remember telling God, "I believe in You, but I need You to show me that You're here. I need provision." And in less than an hour, God answered. This experience reinforced the truth that when Jesus is the Bread of Life, He provides for our needs in ways that we never expect, and often, He answers us in the most unexpected moments. In my moment of desperation, prayer brought immediate results—proof that God is always faithful to provide.

The Spiritual Bread

While Jesus cares about our physical needs, His ultimate provision is spiritual. He is the Bread of Life, offering eternal sustenance. After feeding the 5,000, He taught that the bread He gives leads to eternal life. This invitation calls us beyond our temporary needs to a relationship with Him.

A Call to Trust

The challenge for many of us is learning to trust that Jesus truly is enough. We often look at what we lack instead of what He can provide. Just as the disciples doubted when they saw the small offering of loaves and fish, we may underestimate what God can do with the little we have.

This chapter invites you to bring your "loaves and fish" to Jesus, trusting Him to multiply them for His glory and your good. Whether it's your finances, time, or energy, He can turn scarcity into abundance.

Reflection: What areas of your life feel limited? How can you trust Jesus as the Bread of Life to provide both your physical and spiritual needs? Let this chapter challenge you to shift your perspective and step into His abundant provision.

Chapter 7: Walking on Water

Faith often requires stepping into the unknown. In Matthew 14:22-33, we see Peter boldly walking on water toward Jesus amidst a storm. This miraculous moment teaches us about trust, focus, and the presence of Jesus in life's most turbulent seasons.

The Call to Step Out

After feeding the 5,000, Jesus sent His disciples ahead while He prayed. As their boat struggled against the wind, He walked on the water toward them. In awe and fear, the disciples thought they saw a ghost. But Jesus reassured them, saying, *"Take courage! It is I. Don't be afraid"* (Matthew 14:27).

Peter responded, *"Lord, if it's you, tell me to come to you on the water."* When Jesus said, *"Come,"* Peter stepped out of the boat.

Faith begins with a call. Like Peter, we often find ourselves in situations where Jesus invites us to step into something beyond our abilities.

The Power of Focus

As long as Peter kept his eyes on Jesus, he walked on the water. But when he noticed the wind and waves, fear overtook him, and he began to sink. Jesus immediately reached out, saying, *"You of little faith, why did you doubt?"*

This moment illustrates how easily doubt can disrupt faith. Challenges will arise, but staying focused on Jesus keeps us above the chaos.

Testimony: Walking on Water in Ministry

In September 2023, we began planning the *Jesus Saves Crusade*, set to take place on November 4th. The vision was grand, but the resources were few. At the time, all we had was a tent—no sound equipment, no lighting, and many of our members were facing financial struggles.

To make matters worse, some pastors and elders left the ministry due to the pressure. Those who remained chose to keep the faith, coming together to pray and trust in God's provision.

Week by week, God showed Himself faithful. Donations came from unexpected sources, including non-members who were moved to support us. The crusade was a resounding success. Lives were touched, souls were saved, and Jesus was glorified. Like Peter, we stepped out onto the water, and Jesus carried us through the storm.

A Savior in the Storm

When Peter began to sink, Jesus didn't let him drown. He reached out and saved him. In our storms, Jesus is always near, ready to rescue when we falter.

The storm didn't cease immediately; the lesson was in trusting Jesus' presence, not the absence of trouble.

Your Call to Step Out

What is Jesus calling you to step into? It might be a new opportunity, a ministry, or trusting Him in a difficult situation. Like Peter, you may face fear and doubt, but Jesus is always near, encouraging you to take courage.

Reflection

What "storm" are you facing? How can you refocus on Jesus to overcome fear and doubt? This chapter challenges you to step out of your comfort zone, trusting that Jesus will guide and sustain you, even amidst life's waves.

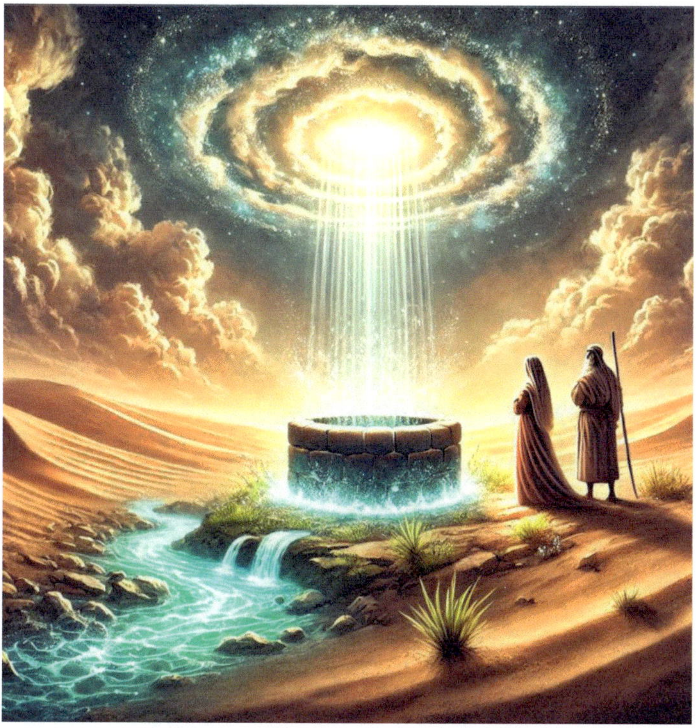

Chapter 8: Living Water

In John 4:13-14, Jesus offers the Samaritan woman at the well a profound gift: **living water** that quenches the soul's thirst forever. This chapter delves into how the living water Jesus provides is a source of eternal life, spiritual satisfaction, and transformation, even for those deemed unworthy by society.

The Encounter at the Well

In the heat of the day, Jesus meets a Samaritan woman drawing water from Jacob's well. She comes alone, likely due to societal rejection. Yet, Jesus breaks cultural barriers by engaging her in conversation, saying:
"Everyone who drinks this water will be thirsty again, but whoever drinks the water I give them will never thirst. Indeed, the water I give them will become in them a spring of water welling up to eternal life" (John 4:13-14).

This encounter reveals Jesus' heart for the outcast and His power to offer eternal satisfaction to every thirsty soul.

Thirst Beyond the Physical

The Samaritan woman's life was marked by unmet longings. Her string of broken relationships reflected a deeper thirst that physical water or worldly pursuits couldn't quench. Jesus' living water represents the fulfillment only He can provide—a relationship with God that restores, renews, and refreshes.

In our lives, we often chase things—success, wealth, approval—that leave us spiritually parched. Jesus invites us to drink from the living water, satisfying our deepest needs.

Testimony: Streams of Living Water in My Life

In my early ministry, there were seasons when I felt unworthy of God's call. I wrestled with feelings of inadequacy, comparing myself to others who seemed more capable or qualified.

One particular moment of doubt stands out. I was preparing to preach on God's faithfulness and couldn't shake the feeling that my past failures disqualified me. I prayed earnestly for reassurance, asking God to show me He was still working through me.

That evening, a member of the congregation approached me, sharing how my previous sermon had profoundly impacted their life. They described it as a "refreshing stream" that revived their hope. This testimony reminded me that God uses the broken and the willing to pour out His living water into others.

Testimony: Streams of Living Water Restoring Relationships

Beyond my personal testimony, I've witnessed the living water of Jesus bring renewal and healing in relationships within our community.
A mother and daughter, estranged for years due to unresolved hurts, found healing and reconciliation through prayer and surrender to Jesus. Their relationship, once filled with pain and silence, now flourishes with love and mutual respect.

Similarly, daughters and their in-laws, as well as sons and their in-laws, moved from tension and misunderstanding to unity and peace. These restorations testify to the power of Jesus' living water—not only to quench our individual thirst but also to refresh and transform broken relationships. When Jesus fills us with His love, it overflows into every aspect of our lives, bringing healing where it seemed impossible and reconciliation where there was division.

Transformation Through Living Water

When the Samaritan woman received the revelation of Jesus as the Messiah, she left her jar behind and ran to tell others. Her shame turned into boldness, and her testimony led many in her village to believe in Jesus (John 4:28-30, 39).

The living water Jesus provides doesn't just quench our own thirst—it overflows, transforming us into vessels of His grace and love for others.

Your Source of Living Water

Are you weary from seeking fulfillment in temporary things? Jesus offers you living water—eternal life and a relationship with God that satisfies your soul and transforms your life. When you drink from His well, you'll never thirst again.

Reflection

- What areas of your life feel dry and unsatisfied?
- How can you draw closer to Jesus, the source of living water?
- Who in your life needs to hear about this life-giving gift?

I encourage you to come to Jesus with your thirst and allow Him to fill you with the water that gives life—abundantly and eternally.

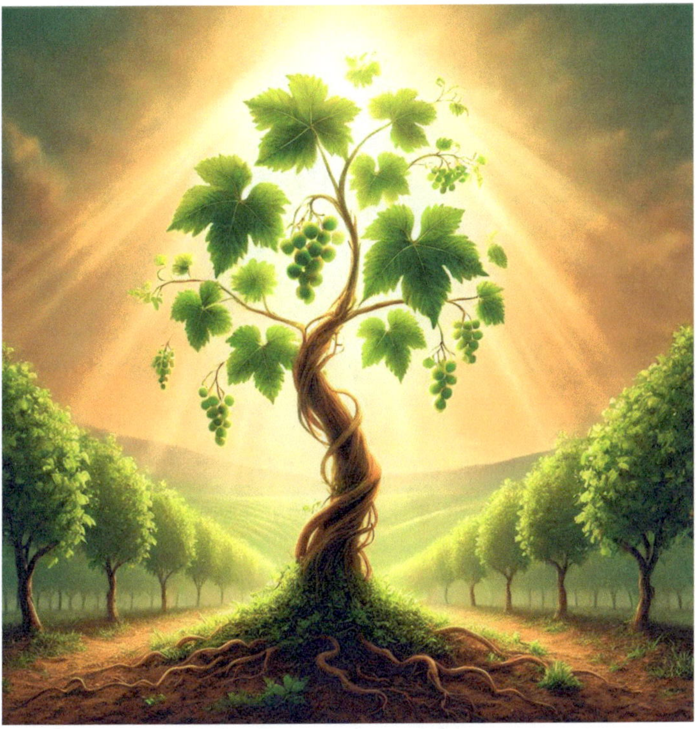

Chapter 9: The Vine and the Branches

In John 15:1-8, Jesus paints a powerful picture of the relationship between Himself and His followers: He is the Vine, and we are the branches. This chapter delves into the vital connection we must maintain with Christ to bear fruit, live purposefully, and glorify God.

Abiding in the Vine

Jesus begins by saying, *"I am the true vine, and my Father is the gardener"* (John 15:1). The imagery is clear: our spiritual life and growth depend on remaining connected to Christ. A branch detached from the vine cannot bear fruit, and neither can we if we drift away from Jesus.

To abide in Christ is to stay in constant fellowship with Him through prayer, worship, and obedience to His Word. It is not about striving, but about surrendering and drawing nourishment from Him.

Pruned to Produce

Jesus also highlights the role of the Father as the gardener:
"Every branch that does bear fruit He prunes so that it will be even more fruitful" (John 15:2).

Pruning involves removing the dead and unproductive parts of our lives—bad habits, distractions, or anything that hinders spiritual growth. Though the process may be painful, it leads to greater fruitfulness and deeper intimacy with Christ.

The Power of Fruitfulness

"If you remain in me and I in you, you will bear much fruit; apart from me, you can do nothing" (John 15:5).

The fruit Jesus refers to is the evidence of a life transformed by Him: love, joy, peace, patience, kindness, goodness, faithfulness, gentleness, and self-control (Galatians 5:22-23).

When we abide in Christ, His life flows through us, enabling us to impact others and glorify God. Fruitfulness is not about what we can achieve in our strength, but about what Christ accomplishes through us.

Testimony: Remaining in the Vine Through Adversity

Through the year 2023-2024, our church faced a season of division. Misunderstandings and disagreements threatened to tear apart the unity we had worked so hard to build. As a leader, I felt overwhelmed and helpless.

In the midst of the chaos, I turned to God in prayer, asking for wisdom and strength. John 15 became a lifeline, reminding me that my role was to remain in Christ, trusting Him to bring healing. Slowly but surely, God began to work in the hearts of the members. Reconciliation replaced bitterness, and unity was restored. Yet, some members left, and that experience was painful. But even in the midst of this, the truth of John 15 echoed louder in my ears, reminding me that abiding in the Vine was crucial.

This season taught me the importance of staying connected to Jesus, especially in the midst of challenges. It also reminded me of a brother in our church who has gone through his own cycles of disconnection. Whenever things are going well for him, he forgets the importance of fellowship and chooses to live a secular life—engaging in drinking and partying. The end result is always tragic.

On two separate occasions, after disconnecting from the Lord, he faced severe consequences. The first time, he lost important destiny helpers, and his business closed down. The second time, after the Lord had restored him, he lost his car and business equipment. Each time, his life was affected because he had strayed from the Vine, and in the absence of connection to Christ, the fruit of his labor withered.

This experience—both in my own life and in witnessing the consequences of disconnection—reinforced the truth that staying connected to Jesus is the key to navigating adversity and bearing lasting fruit in ministry and life. When we remain in Him, no matter the storm, we can trust that He will provide what we need to endure and grow.

The Glory of the Gardener

Jesus concludes with a powerful statement: ***"This is to my Father's glory, that you bear much fruit, showing yourselves to be my disciples"*** (John 15:8).

The ultimate purpose of our fruitfulness is to glorify God. As we grow and bear fruit, our lives become a testimony of His power and grace, drawing others to Him.

Your Connection to the Vine

Are you abiding in the Vine, or have you been trying to bear fruit on your own? Jesus invites you to remain in Him, trusting Him to provide all you need for a life of purpose and impact.

Reflection
- What areas of your life need pruning?
- How can you strengthen your connection to Jesus daily?

- Who in your life needs to experience the fruit of God's love through you?

In this chapter I hope you are challenged to prioritize your relationship with Christ, knowing that apart from Him, you can do nothing. Abide in the Vine and let His life flow through you to bless others and glorify God.

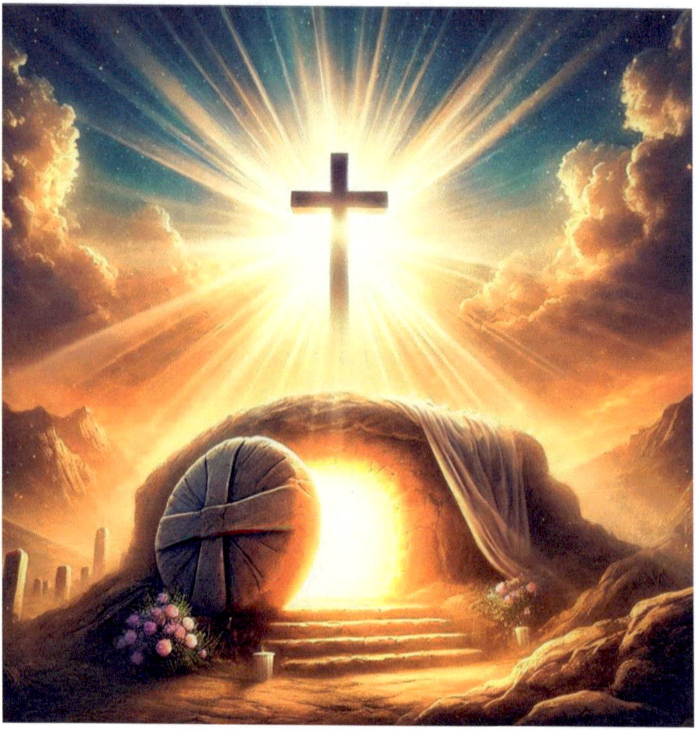

Chapter 10: The Power of the Resurrection

The resurrection of Jesus Christ is the heartbeat of the Christian faith, the cornerstone of our hope, and the source of all spiritual strength. It is a living, breathing power that permeates every part of our Christian walk, transforming us and empowering us to live victoriously. The resurrection is not just an event in history; it is the foundation of our hope, the victory over sin and death, and the ultimate source of strength for every believer.

In this chapter, we will dig deeply into the significance of the resurrection, its power in our lives today, and how we can live in its transformative reality.

The Victory of the Cross

The death of Jesus on the cross was not the end but the beginning of an extraordinary victory. Jesus willingly laid down His life, paying the price for our sins. But death could not hold Him; He conquered it. As Paul wrote in 1 Corinthians 15:20, "But Christ has indeed been raised from the dead, the firstfruits of those who have fallen asleep." Jesus' resurrection marks the first of many to come, as He offers us the same victory over death.

The cross of Jesus Christ is often seen as a symbol of sacrifice, pain, and suffering.

But it is also a symbol of victory.

Jesus' death on the cross was not a defeat; it was a powerful moment in God's divine plan of redemption. Through His death, Jesus took the weight of our sins upon Himself, providing a perfect sacrifice for humanity. But that was not the end. As we read in 1 Corinthians 15:55-57: "Where, O death, is your victory? Where, O death, is your sting? The sting of death is sin, and the power of sin is the law. But thanks be to God! He gives us the victory through our Lord Jesus Christ."

The resurrection is the proof of that victory. Death was conquered, sin was defeated, and the power of the enemy was broken. As the firstborn from the dead, Jesus paves the way for all believers to experience that same victory over sin, death, and the grave. His resurrection is a victory cry that echoes through eternity, affirming that He has defeated everything that stands in the way of our relationship with God.

A New Beginning

The resurrection signifies new life. For Jesus, it was the triumph over the grave; for us, it is the promise of new beginnings. Jesus said in John 11:25, "I am the resurrection and the life. The one who believes in me will live, even though they die." When we accept Christ, we are spiritually resurrected, and we are given the opportunity for a new life in Him.

The resurrection of Jesus is not only a historic event but also a present reality for those who follow Him. When Jesus rose from the dead, He demonstrated that the power of God could bring life out of death, hope out of despair, and light out of darkness. This is the promise He offers to us all: that through His resurrection, we too can experience new life.

As Jesus said in John 11:25-26: "I am the resurrection and the life. The one who believes in me will live, even though they die; and whoever lives by believing in me will never die." This promise goes beyond the physical realm; it speaks to the transformation of our hearts and spirits. Through His resurrection, we are invited into a relationship with God that not only impacts our eternal future but also brings life to our present circumstances.

In Romans 6:4, Paul explains, "We were therefore buried with him through baptism into death in order that, just as Christ was raised from the dead through the glory of the Father, we too may live a new life."

The resurrection means that we have been spiritually resurrected with Christ, and this new life empowers us to live in ways that glorify God. It is a new beginning, one where we are no longer bound by the chains of sin and death but are free to live in the fullness of God's grace.

Testimony: New Life in Christ

In my own life, I have witnessed the resurrection power of Christ time and again. In my early ministry, I faced many obstacles—both internal and external—that threatened to stop me from fulfilling God's call on my life. There were times I felt spiritually dead, weighed down by my own failures and doubts. But each time, God reminded me that the resurrection wasn't just an event to be remembered; it was a power to be experienced.

I remember a particularly challenging season in 2024, when my ministry was going through a rough patch. We were struggling financially, and some of the people close to me had fallen away from the faith. On top of that, my family and I were under attack in our health. The burden felt overwhelming. I remember feeling physically drained and spiritually exhausted, asking myself if I could continue in the work God had called me to do.

But God, in His mercy and faithfulness, reminded me of the power of the resurrection. He told me that no matter the difficulties, I could trust in His ability to bring life into dead situations. In the midst of these trials, I turned to God in prayer, seeking His strength and guidance.

One particular moment stands out in my memory. On Sunday, October 20, 2024, I had made a covenant with God in prayer and promised to minister, regardless of my condition. That week, I had suffered a severe back injury on Wednesday, and by Sunday, I could barely stand up straight. The pain was excruciating, and I had been prescribed painkillers by my doctor, but I knew I had a responsibility to preach.

In faith, I stood up to minister, trusting that God would meet me in my weakness. And in that very moment, as I stood to go preach, the pain left me instantly. I had never felt it again after that service. It was as though the power of the resurrection had entered my body and brought healing. That moment was a powerful reminder that God's resurrection power is not just for the future but for today. He is alive, and He is still in the business of performing miracles.

This experience was not only a physical healing but a deep spiritual renewal for me. God showed me that the resurrection power of Jesus is present in every area of our lives—our health, our finances, our relationships, and our ministries. It is the same power that raised Christ from the dead, and it is available to us now.

Walking in Resurrection Power

When we embrace the resurrection, we are called to walk in its power daily. This doesn't just mean waiting for heaven; it means living a life of victory over sin, fear, and despair here on earth. Paul says in Romans 8:11, "And if the Spirit of him who raised Jesus from the dead is living in you, he who raised Christ from the dead will also give life to your mortal bodies because of his Spirit who lives in you."
The power of the resurrection is available to all believers. It is the strength that enables us to overcome temptation, live righteously, and boldly proclaim the gospel.

To walk in the resurrection power of Jesus is to live in victory over the things that seek to keep us bound. It means recognizing that because Jesus conquered the grave, we too can overcome every challenge and hardship.

Living in resurrection power means that we are no longer slaves to fear, sin, or hopelessness. We have been given the power of the Holy Spirit to live with boldness, purpose, and joy, knowing that no weapon formed against us will prosper (Isaiah 54:17). We are empowered to fulfill the mission God has placed on our lives and to bring hope to a world that desperately needs it.

The Resurrection: Our Daily Victory

When we consider the resurrection, we often think of it as a future hope—something to look forward to in the life to come. And certainly, the resurrection is our ultimate hope for eternity.

But the power of the resurrection is not just for the future; it is a present reality.
It empowers us to live victoriously today, to walk in holiness, to resist temptation, and to fulfill God's calling on our lives.

In Philippians 3:10-11, Paul writes, "I want to know Christ—yes, to know the power of his resurrection and participation in his sufferings, becoming like him in his death, and so, somehow, attaining to the resurrection from the dead." Paul's desire was to experience the power of the resurrection in his daily life. He knew that this power was the key to living a life of joy, purpose, and effectiveness in the kingdom of God.

As believers, we are called to walk in this power. The resurrection is not just a theological concept; it is a living force that transforms us from the inside out. It is the power that enables us to forgive when it's hard, to love when it's difficult, to serve when we feel tired, and to persevere when we are tempted to give up.

Your Resurrection Power

Is there an area of your life that feels dead or lifeless? Is there a relationship that needs resurrection, a ministry that seems stagnant, or a heart that feels empty? Jesus, the resurrected Savior, offers you the power to bring life into every dead thing. He offers you His resurrection power to overcome every obstacle and to live the life He has called you to live.

Through the resurrection, Jesus calls us to experience the fullness of life. In Him, we are more than conquerors (Romans 8:37). We are no longer victims of our circumstances but victors in Christ.

I pray for you to experience the resurrection power of our Lord Jesus at your point of need. In Jesus Name. Amen

Reflection

- In what areas of your life do you need to experience the power of Jesus' resurrection?
- How can you walk in the victory of the resurrection daily?

- Who can you share the power of the resurrection with today?

I challenge you to reflect on the hope and power that comes through the resurrection of Jesus Christ. His victory is our victory. His life is our life. Through Him, we have the power to live as overcomers.

Made in the USA
Columbia, SC
23 January 2025